# 15 CHART HITS
## FOR PIANO SOLO

ISBN 978-1-70517-716-7

Visit Hal Leonard Online at
**www.halleonard.com**

World headquarters, contact:
**Hal Leonard**
7777 West Bluemound Road
Milwaukee, WI 53213
Email: info@halleonard.com

In Europe, contact:
**Hal Leonard Europe Limited**
1 Red Place
London, W1K 6PL
Email: info@halleonardeurope.com

In Australia, contact:
**Hal Leonard Australia Pty. Ltd.**
4 Lentara Court
Cheltenham, Victoria, 3192 Australia
Email: info@halleonard.com.au

# ALL TOO WELL

Words and Music by TAYLOR SWIFT
and LIZ ROSE

Moderately

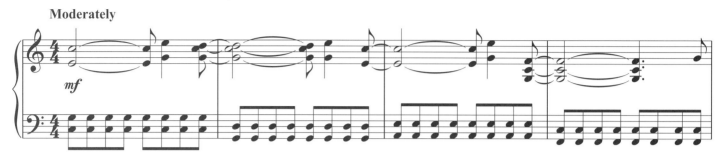

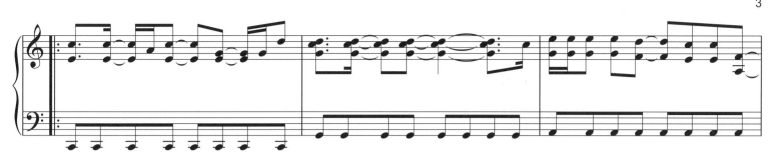

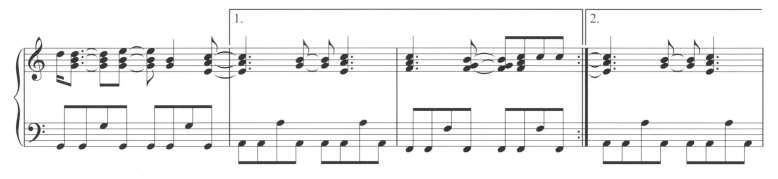

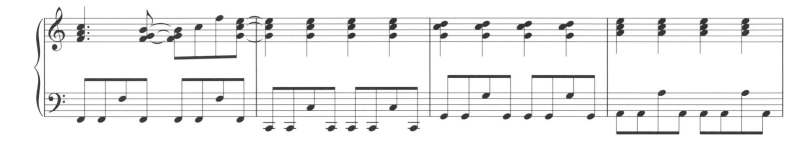

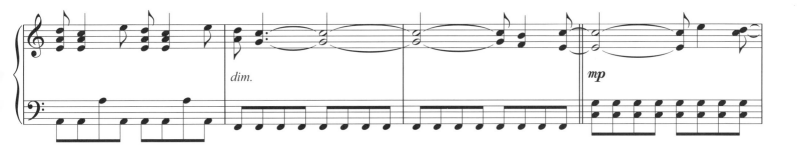

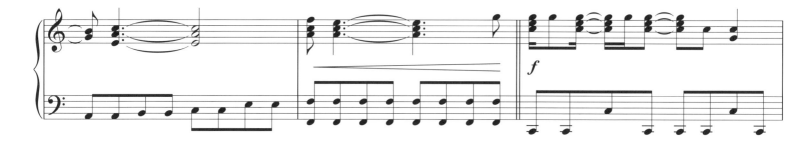

# BAD HABITS

Words and Music by ED SHEERAN,
JOHNNY McDAID and FRED GIBSON

Moderately fast

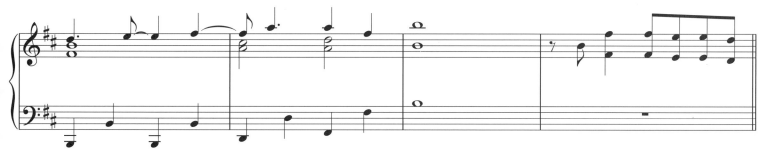

# AS IT WAS

Words and Music by HARRY STYLES,
THOMAS HULL and TYLER JOHNSON

Moderately fast

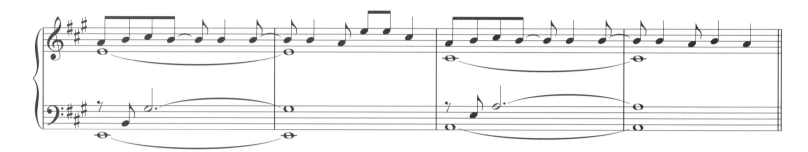

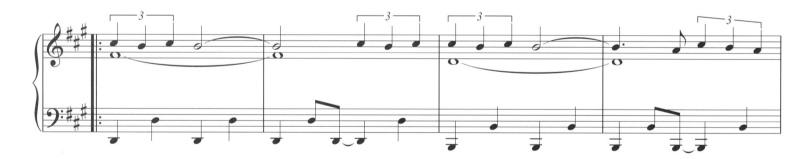

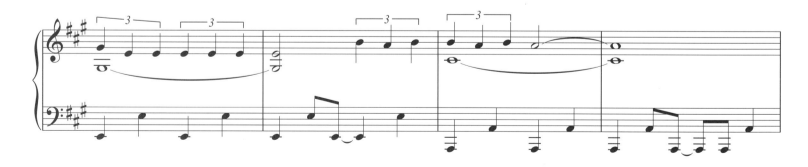

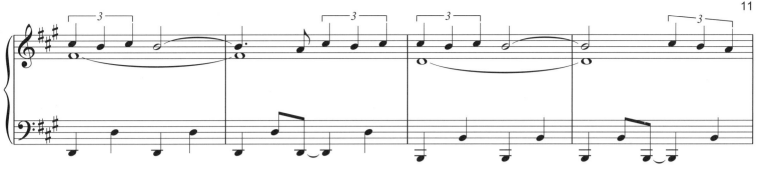

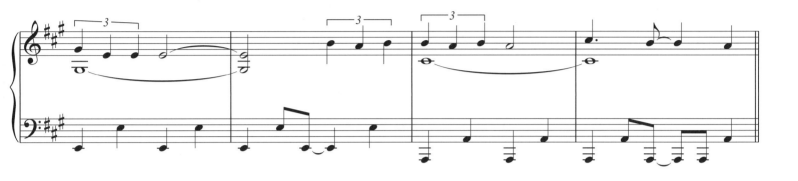

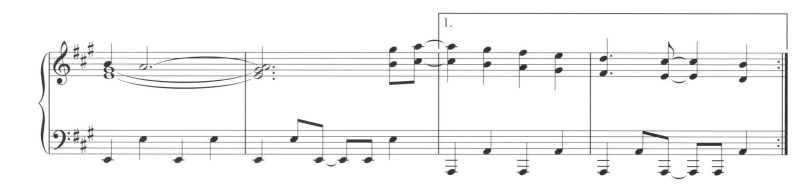

# BLINDING LIGHTS

Words and Music by ABEL TESFAYE,
MAX MARTIN, JASON QUENNEVILLE,
OSCAR HOLTER and AHMAD BALSHE

**Fast Dance tempo**

To Coda ⊕

D.C. al Coda
(no repeat)

CODA
⊕

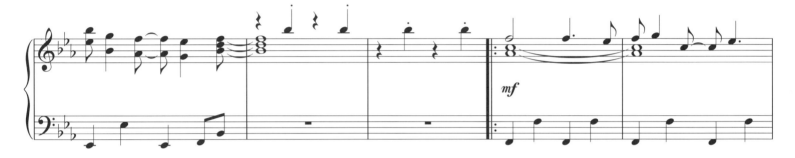

# DRIVERS LICENSE

Words and Music by OLIVIA RODRIGO
and DANIEL NIGRO

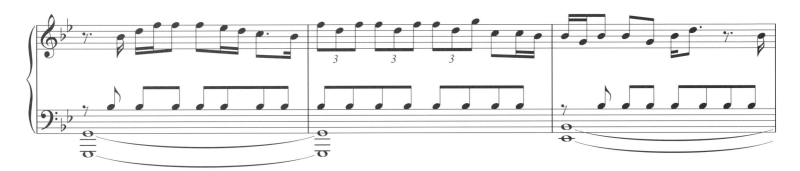

# COVER ME IN SUNSHINE

Words and Music by MAUREEN McDONALD
and AMY ALLEN

**Moderately, in 2**

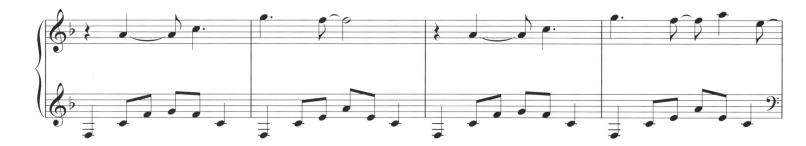

# EASY ON ME

Words and Music by ADELE ADKINS
and GREG KURSTIN

# GLIMPSE OF US

Words and Music by JOJI KUSUNOKI,
CONNOR McDONOUGH, RILEY McDONOUGH,
JOEL CASTILLO and ALEXIS KESSELMAN

Moderately slow, in 2

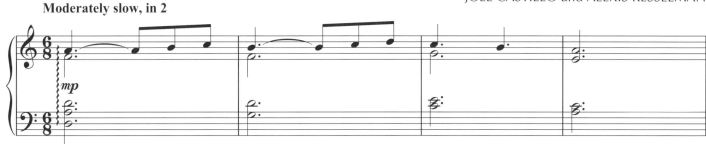

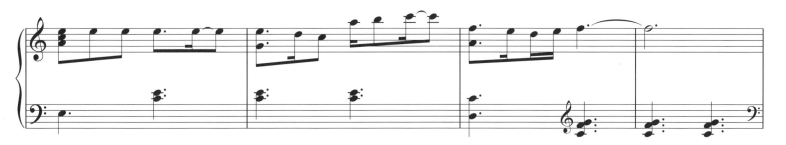

**To Coda** ⊕

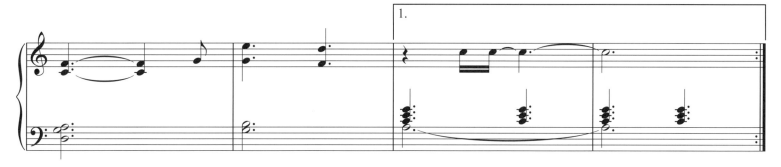

# HOLD MY HAND

### from TOP GUN: MAVERICK

Words and Music by STEFANI GERMANOTTA
and MICHAEL TUCKER

**Power Ballad**

# NO TIME TO DIE
## from NO TIME TO DIE

Words and Music by BILLIE EILISH O'CONNELL
and FINNEAS O'CONNELL

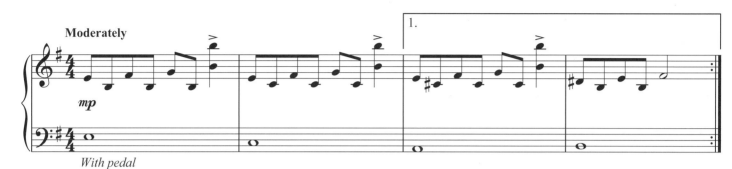

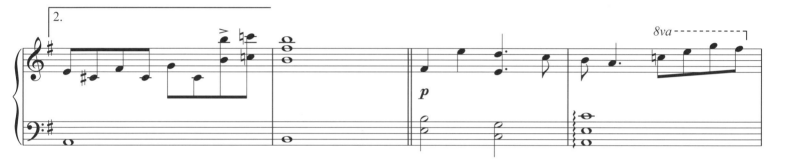

# MEMORIES

Words and Music by ADAM LEVINE,
JONATHAN BELLION, JORDAN JOHNSON,
JACOB HINDLIN, STEFAN JOHNSON,
MICHAEL POLLACK and VINCENT FORD

**Relaxed groove**

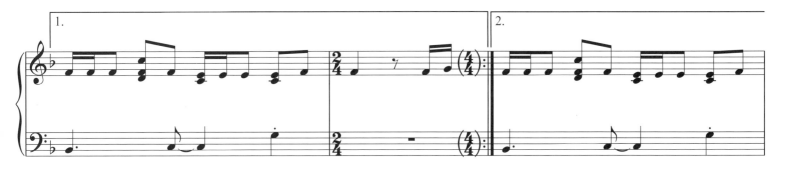

# ON MY WAY

## from MARRY ME

Words and Music by LEROY JAMES CLAMPITT,
IVY ADARA and MICHAEL POLLACK

**Slow Ballad**

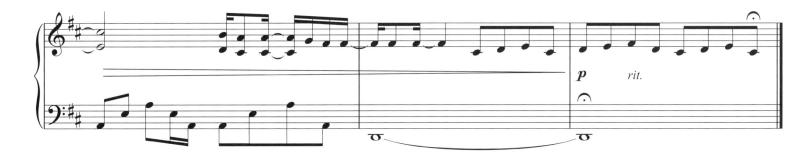

# SEÑORITA

Words and Music by CAMILA CABELLO,
CHARLOTTE AITCHISON, JACK PATTERSON,
SHAWN MENDES, MAGNUS HØIBERG,
BENJAMIN LEVIN, ALI TAMPOSI
and ANDREW WOTMAN

**Moderate Latin groove**

44

**To Coda** $\oplus$

# SPEECHLESS
### from ALADDIN

Music by ALAN MENKEN
Lyrics by BENJ PASEK
and JUSTIN PAUL

**Moderately slow, in 2**

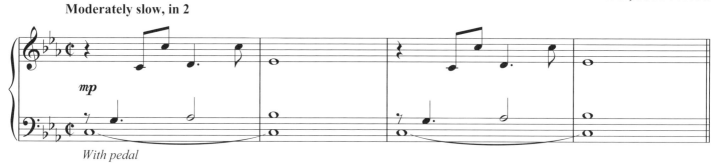

*mp*

*With pedal*

48

To Coda 

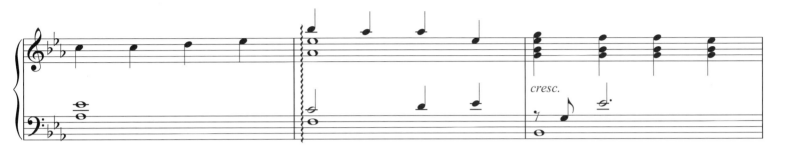

# WE DON'T TALK ABOUT BRUNO

### from ENCANTO

Music and Lyrics by
LIN-MANUEL MIRANDA

Moderately

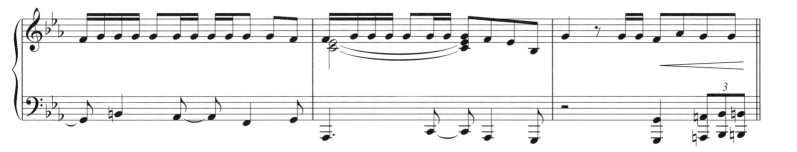

*p* sub.

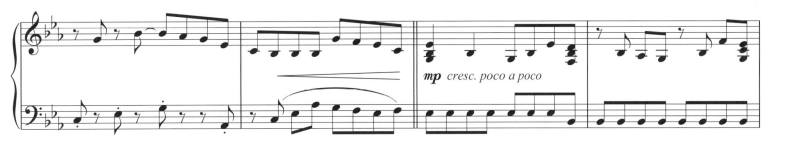

# More Songbooks from Your Favorite Artists

## ADELE – 30

12 songs: All Night Parking (Interlude) • Can I Get It • Can't Be Together • Cry Your Heart Out • Easy on Me • Hold On • I Drink Wine • Love Is a Game • My Little Love • Oh My God • Strangers by Nature • To Be Loved • Wild Wild West • Woman like Me.

00396758  Piano/Vocal/Guitar ..................................................$19.99

## JUSTIN BIEBER – JUSTICE

15 songs: Anyone • Die for You • Hold On • Holy • Lonely • Love You Different • Peaches • Somebody • Unstable • and more.

00368491  Piano/Vocal/Guitar ..................................................$19.99

## COLDPLAY – EVERYDAY LIFE

16 tracks featuring the title track plus: Arabesque • Broken • Champion of the World • Church • Cry Cry Cry • Daddy • Eko • Guns • Sunrise • When I Need a Friend • and more.

00327962  Piano/Vocal/Guitar ..................................................$19.99

## BILLIE EILISH – HAPPIER THAN EVER

15 songs: Billie Bossa Nova • Everybody Dies • Getting Older • Lost Cause • My Future • NDA • Therefore I Am • Your Power • and more.

00369297  Piano/Vocal/Guitar ..................................................$19.99

## FOO FIGHTERS – GREATEST HITS

15 songs: All My Life • Best of You • Big Me • Breakout • Everlong • Learn to Fly • Long Road to Ruin • Monkey Wrench • My Hero • The Pretender • Skin and Bones • This Is a Call • Times like These • Wheels • Word Forward • and more.

00142501  Piano/Vocal/Guitar..................................................$22.99

## ARIANA GRANDE – THANK U, NEXT

11 songs: Bad Idea • Bloodline • Break up with Your Girlfriend, I'm Bored • Fake Smile • Ghostin • Imagine • In My Head • Make Up • NASA • Needy • 7 Rings.

00292769  Piano/Vocal/Guitar ..................................................$19.99

## SHAWN MENDES – WONDER

14 songs: Always Been You • Call My Friends • Can't Imagine • Dream • Higher • Intro • Look up at the Stars • Monster • Piece of You • Song for No One • Teach Me How to Love • 305 • 24 Hours • Wonder.

00363568  Piano/Vocal/Guitar ..................................................$19.99

## MAREN MORRIS – SHEET MUSIC COLLECTION

15 songs: The Bones • Craving You • Dear Hate • 80s Mercedes • Girl • I Could Use a Love Song • The Middle • My Church • Rich • A Song for Everything • and more.

00319925  Piano/Vocal/Guitar ..................................................$19.99

## OLIVIA RODRIGO – SOUR

11 songs: Brutal • Deja Vu • Drivers License • Enough for You • Good 4 U • Happier • Hope Ur OK • Jealousy, Jealousy • Traitor • and more.

00369986  Piano/Vocal/Guitar ..................................................$19.99

## HARRY STYLES – HARRY'S HOUSE

13 songs: As It Was • Boyfriends • Cinema • Daydreaming • Daylight • Grapejuice • Keep Driving • Late Night Talking • Little Freak • Love of My Life • Matilda • Music for a Sushi Restaurant • Satellite.

01060060  Piano/Vocal/Guitar..................................................$19.99

## TAYLOR SWIFT – RED (TAYLOR'S VERSION)

29 songs: All Too Well (both versions!) • Better Man • Everything Has Changed • Holy Ground • I Knew You Were Trouble • Red • Sad Beautiful Tragic • State of Grace • 22 • We Are Never Ever Getting Back Together • and more.

00394706  Piano/Vocal/Guitar .................................................. $27.99

For a complete listing of the products available, visit us online at **www.halleonard.com**

*Contents, prices, and availability subject to change without notice.*